WE CHALLENGE YOU TO...

1. Visit one of the twelve fantastic pubs/restaurants in this book

2. Enjoy a slap-up meal

3. Try to recreate their chosen recipe back at home

4. Share your results on Instagram @thechefschallenge
& Facebook 'The Chef's Challenge'

But, most importantly, have fun! And take pride in helping to rejuvinate our local hospitality industry after a very difficult year.

FEATURING...

THE CRICKETERS, ASH GREEN

THE GEORGE, KELVEDON

THE HALF BUTT, GREAT HORKSLEY

NORTH HILL NOODLE BAR, COLCHESTER

THE ANGEL, KELVEDON

KINGSFORD PARK, COLCHESTER

THE FORESTERS, COLCHESTER

THE SWAN, LONG MELFORD

THE MANGER, BRADFIELD COMBUST

STATION ROAD, SUDBURY

THE CROWN, STOKE BY NAYLAND

THE GRANARY, WALDEGRAVES

WELCOME TO THE CHEF'S CHALLENGE...

Hello, my name is Jason Cattrell and I love cooking. I'm an author, a foodie, and I also have a small business distributing cooking oil to restaurants, hotels, hospitals, schools etc., which is great because I get to chat with the chefs and pick up lots of tips.

One of the things I like to do most is to try and recreate at home some the amazing dishes that I see going through 'The Pass'. I don't always succeed, because I'm not a trained chef, but I get pretty close sometimes.

I have put this book together because I think lots of people out there are just like me; they love to cook and try new dishes, and love eating out and finding inspiration. But I also created this book because I want to encourage people to get out there and support our local restaurants after a very difficult 2020. Hopefully, the Chef's Challenge is a fun way that we can do that together.

The Chef's Challenge is for food lovers who like to try new things. It is a simple concept – twelve chefs from around Essex and Suffolk have put forward twelve dishes for you to enjoy at their venues and try to recreate at home.

We all love to eat out. It is easier than cooking at home, we can socialise and, frankly, the chefs are professionals and can do what we can't because they are trained; they are the unsung heroes of our evenings out.

This is not a recipe book, although there are twelve recipes in it. Nor is it about creating picture-perfect versions of those recipes. This is a book of fun challenges and mini adventures, which will encourage you get to go out to the twelve venues, try the chefs' chosen dishes, absorb the aroma of the food, the taste, the presentation and then try to recreate those dishes at home.

When you've cooked your dish, post your results, successes and failures (we can't be perfect all of the time) on Instagram, so that we can join in the fun together. You could even challenge your friends and family to take part too, and compare your results!

We are all at different levels of skill in our cooking, so these dishes range from fairly easy and well presented to a bit more complicated but doable at home with some extra effort. With twelve to choose from, you can have a foodie adventure every month throughout the year and discover venues that you haven't visited before. At the end of the year, you'll have twelve great dishes of food under your belt that, as a cook, you can knock out whenever you want to.

Now, chefs do move around, and venues change recipes seasonally, so if this happens our venues will put the Chef's Challenge logo by the new dish and will keep a typed list of ingredients and instructions for you to follow. You might end up with a surprise dish to try out and to cook at home!

Here is my extra challenge to you: make it yours.

Make the dish yours by adding your own twist to it, be that an extra garnish, a different herb or spice, or even an extra side dish. Take what you see and taste and then add a little extra if you want to. If you can't find the exact ingredients then improvise, it's okay to experiment.

A big thing to remember is that we don't always get it right, and that's okay. I have had my fair share of disasters and unexpected troubles, as you will see on the Instagram page, and I try to learn from every mistake or messed up preconception. I mean, who knew you could actually eat lemon rinds? (Thanks to the Atchar Chef Mathew Scully.)

My last thought to you is that cooking is a never-ending adventure. There are so many amazing and simple dishes to try out from all over the world. Sometimes we get them right, sometimes not, but it is a true voyage of fun and discovery. And I hope you'll find a little of that within these pages.

D. J. Cattrell

THE
CHEF'S CHALLENGE

Out of all of the venues that I service, 'The Cricketers' at Eight Ash Green is one of my favourites. Not because it is high class fine dining, but because the people who run it are just lovely and the food is always absolutely spot on. It is a proper country pub that is hugely popular with the locals and attracts people from outside of its demographic because of its friendliness and its food, particularly its food. The menu changes seasonally but caters for everyone from vegans to coeliacs and meat eaters. It always provides very well-presented dishes that delight the pallet. And you best take a good appetite with you because they don't stint on portion sizes!

The first chef up to the pass is Mick.

Mick is an ex-military chef who is highly organised, strict and yet very friendly with his staff; he has a wonderfully dry sense of humour. Talking of the staff, this is a family run pub and you really get that feeling when you go there. Julie and Derek have run the pub for fifteen years with their son Matt as a labour of love, and it is a true family gem of Colchester. The pub's car park is always full and the pub has such a great vibe. When the pandemic hit, rather than hunkering down and furloughing everyone, the Cricketers quickly put together a takeaway and delivery service and opened their car park to the local constabulary for free. This is a proper community pub and is well loved by the locals.

THE CHEF

Mick (Michael Illingworth) joined the army in 1976 at the age of eighteen. He always had an interest in cooking, so it was easy for him to choose to become a chef in the army. Being in the Army was a great experience and allowed him to travel to countries that he would not otherwise have been able to visit at that age. He got to experience food from far flung places such as Hong Kong and, closer to home, in Northern Ireland. He even had the honour of being part of a catering team that has cooked for members of the royal family.

He left the army in 1988 and joined the prison service in 1989, serving at Pentonville and Chelmsford prisons. He left there in 2007 after eighteen years of service. He then went to the Thatcher's Arms in Mount Bures where he was nominated for pub chef of the year, making the final three.

Mick joined the Cricketers in 2012, taking on the role of head chef. He and his catering team have built up a great reputation for producing excellent home cooked meals and daily specials, and they endeavour to use local produce from suppliers in Colchester.

Him and his lovely spouse Eileen have been together for eighteen years. The also have four lovely grandchildren, aged from five months to thirteen years, so life is always busy!

THE DISH

Monkfish wrapped in Parma ham with butter sautéed potatoes, asparagus, roasted cherry tomatoes and a sambuca sauce.

(When cooking this, like many dishes, the star of the show is the sauce. That sambuca sauce just tingles the tongue. When I tried to recreate it, I added just a few chilli flakes to the sauce as my twist on this dish.)

INGREDIENTS (Serves 4)

4 x 6oz monkfish tails

8 slices of Parma ham

1 tin chopped tomatoes

1 small red onion

12 asparagus tips

1kg large potatoes

Cherry tomatoes on the vine

Sambuca

1 lemon

Salt & pepper

PREPARATION

Wrap the monkfish tails with Parma ham, then wrap each one in cling film. Place in fridge. This can be done in advance.

Peel potatoes and cut up into ¾ inch dice, then par boil for 5 mins. Strain and allow to cool. This can also be done in advance.

Peel and dice the red onion and fry for 2 minutes or until the onion is soft, add chopped tomatoes and salt and pepper. Bring to the boil and simmer for 15 mins. Add sambuca and bring back to the boil. Liquidise the onions and tomatoes to make the sauce.

All the above can be done well in advance to make things easier.

METHOD

Heat some oil in a non-stick pan. Place the monkfish in the pan and cook for 2 minutes each side. Place on a baking tray and cook for 18 minutes at 180°C

Heat some more oil in another frying pan and fry the diced potatoes until golden brown, add salt and pepper. Place on a baking tray and cook for 15 minutes.

Roast the cherry vine tomatoes for 10 minutes, making sure you have brushed with oil and salt and pepper.

Sauté the asparagus in a little butter on a medium heat, being careful not to burn the butter.

Serve with the Sambuca sauce.

VISIT THE CRICKETERS

Spring Ln, Fordham Heath, Eight Ash Green, Colchester CO3 9TG

www.thecricketerscolchester.co.uk

NOW IT'S YOUR TURN!

Cook Mick's 'Monkfish Wrapped In Parma Ham' and upload a picture of your dish to Instagram @thechefschallenge.

Next up... THE GEORGE.

If you ever get to meet Gareth (not during service, he'll be too busy) you will meet a man whose looks belie his nature. Frankly he looks like a gangster. But he is in fact one of the nicest guys I have had the privilege to serve over the years. His skills as a chef are beyond question, and the dish that he offers for you to replicate is one that you will no doubt be making over and over again.

I have serviced The George for many years and seen many incumbents come and go, but a few months ago I had a call from an old friend of mine, Chef Gareth. He told me that The George was now in the safe pair of hands of his boss Joey, and asked if I would like to supply them with cooking oil?

Gareth has moved around a lot, picking up skills and helping out places that needed helping out. As long as I have known Gareth, he has been a fixer; a menu trouble shooter. He has designed new menus for different venues and turned those businesses around by offering the right food for that venue. Gareth is what is termed as a consummate professional!

Although Joey only recently took over the George, with Gareth on board he is pretty much guaranteed a successful business; a brave move to take on a restaurant/pub during these Covid times for sure.

Another thing that I love about Gareth is his attention to detail. Here, he has not only given you a list of ingredients but also instructions on how to prepare those ingredients. He then takes you through each step as if he were teaching his sous chef how to prepare the dish. I mean, how amazing is that?! I love this dish.

THE CHEF

Gareth trained at Brands Hatch Hotel and Spa, a two rosette serving traditional French and modern European cuisine.

His first Head Chef job aged 24 was at the George and dragon in Mountnessing, serving English and European food in a large volume gastro restaurant (now that is high pressure cooking!)

From there went to The Brandy Hole at Hullbridge, a fish and seafood restaurant, as Head Chef. Then to Bridge Street Lounge and Grill (where I met him first). He stayed there for two years as Head Chef, serving fine dining food.

From there he took a job as the sous chef at Le Benaix, a French style restaurant in Rettendon.

In January of this year, he joined Lovejoy's Catering and Events (formerly Roamers Caterers) as Head Chef for the events side. Post Covid lockdown,

Lovejoy's invested in the George at Kelvedon, which he then took over as Head Chef, running both sides of the company alongside each other.

THE DISH

Pork tenderloin with seasonal vegetables on a sweet red cabbage puree.

INGREDIENTS & PREPARATION

Pork Tenderloin: trim off the fat and leave only the pure meat for the best results.

Red Cabbage puree: in a pan add onions, garlic and thyme, sweat down slightly. Thinly slice the red cabbage, removing all root. Braise slowly in a pan with red wine and demerara sugar. Add a spoon of butter and a pinch of salt. Once all liquid has reduced, blitz the cabbage with the onion, garlic and thyme until it is a smooth puree. Allow to cool.

Baby turnips : trim off the leaves of the turnips, keep these as they can be used as a pesto or fried as a garnish if desired.

Baby carrots: personally, I love the colours that these provide. By tradition it was actually purple carrots that were served the correct way, it was the Dutch that changed them to being orange. Wash these and trim the leaves off. They can be used again for garnish if you would like.

Baby courgettes: make sure you wash these as well.

Sage : remove leaves from storks. In a hot deep fat fryer (155 degrees) fry for about 2-3 mins or until they become crisp. Leave to drain on a paper towel and lightly salt.

Red wine jus: whilst in a professional kitchen, we use the bones of the animals to make the stock itself

which takes roughly 24-30 hours of cooking and looking after. But in supermarkets, they sell beef or chicken stock pre-made. To make it into red wine jus, I reduce the stock with rosemary sticks, onion, garlic, red wine, balsamic vinegar and port. This is complete once it is able to coat the back of a spoon.

Pork puffs: take the pork skin and remove all fat, leaving the rind by itself. Dry this out at a low temperature for 24 hours. Blitz the crackling to form small shards. Then put into a hot deep fat fryer (180+) until it puffs and becomes little crackling balls. Drain on a towel and lightly season.

METHOD

First thing to do is get your pan lovely and hot. Season your meat with salt and white pepper. Seal each side of the tenderloin off in the pain. Once each side has colour, add in a clove of garlic, three sprigs of thyme and a knob of butter. Once the butter is hot and foaming, using a spoon, I baste over the pork. When the butter is foaming, I add my courgettes, carrots and turnips into the pan. With the turnips I will cut them in half as the inside has a beautiful colour once cooked this way.

From here, I place all the items onto a tray and place them into a preheated oven (200 degrees) for 6 minutes.

At this time, I will take the courgettes and the turnips out and place them on a resting tray. These

are ready for service or can be done in advance if you choose to or are doing a larger party.

The tray goes back into the oven with the pork and the carrots for a further 6 minutes to finish cooking.

In this time, I would put another pan on a low heat, add some salt, butter and a little honey to glaze the carrots into. I find honey better to glaze the carrots in as it has a more subtle taste than sugar and is already smooth, therefore, will not leave a grainy texture to the carrots.

Always leave your meat to rest for 5-6 minutes after you have cooked it, this allows the meat time to relax and the blood to go back into it.

During this time, I would heat my jus, and set myself ready to plate up.

The red cabbage puree, I always serve at room temperature. I find as I always use hot plates, it allows it more than enough time to warm up without drying up on the plate.

First off, I make a splash on the plate with the puree. Following this, I like to cut the purple carrot in half to show the colour mix on the in-side, I will then place it on the plate, using this as my guide I choose where the other cooked vegetables look best on the plate.

Once all the vegetables are on the plate, I cut the pork tenderloin in half lengthways. It should show a medium-well cooking inside which is perfect. I will place the pork on the plate with the centre showing, then use the jus to glaze around the plate and add another dimension to it. Place the crispy sage around along with the crackling puff and you are ready to serve.

A lot of the plating comes from looking at the actual dish, and personally deciding where each new item on the dish should be placed next. I always allow the chefs I work with to come forward with new ideas or ways we could plate something. To me uniqueness is a quality we should all have

VISIT THE GEORGE

Coggeshall Rd, Colchester CO5 9PL

www.thegeorgeatkelvedon.co.uk

NOW IT'S YOUR TURN!

Cook Gareth's 'Pork Tenderloin' and upload picture of your dish to Instagram @thechefschallenge.

Next up... THE HALF BUTT

TIPS FOR COOKING AT HOME

As an obsessive cook, the one thing I have learned to do is to take my time with a dish. For me, it should be like a piece of art, and I want to make sure that get every element right. I don't always, but that's the fun of it!

Preparation is everything; I like to get anything that I can cook before hand, like sauces or even a simple mash, done and ready just to heat up before serving, so that I can concentrate on the trickier stuff.

The most important thing for me, though, is to enjoy the art of cooking and the smiles on the faces of my friends and family when they try a dish that I have prepared.

Why not share pictures of your taste testers' smiles on our Instagram page @thechefschallenge?

The next Chef up to the pass is Lucas.

The Half Butt is special to me as it is my local pub. It was taken over, after many years of struggling to stay afloat, by Becki Churchman. Becki herself is a local lady, and wow has she turned the fortunes of that pub around.

Becki has all the social skills that you want in a landlady; warm, friendly, humorous and welcoming. With the help of Lucas and his menu, the two of them are a winning team that have turned the pub and its food into a successful business as well as a delight to eat at. Another proper family pub.

THE CHEF

Lucas (Lucasz Wiland) was born in Bydgoszcs. In Poland, he trained at a catering college, but grew his love for food from watching and helping his mother. Plus he really loves eating great food, which is what his mother insisted on: quality over quantity. So, naturally, he now likes to experiment with healthy foods.

Lukasz came to England in 2005 to work as a kitchen porter and then a commis chef, firstly to improve his language skills but also to improve his knowledge as a chef. He quickly rose up the ranks by making very simple food taste and look amazing, and he ended up being Head Chef for several restaurants.

He now enjoys creating and making his own dishes, having been made sole chef at the Half Butt, which was placed in the top twenty favourite restaurants during the Government's Eat Out to Help Out Scheme in north Essex. So, hats off to Lucasz.

THE DISH

Rack of ribs in homemade BBQ sauce with sweet potato wedges.

INGREDIENTS

2 x pork loin ribs (ask your butcher for 'baby back ribs')
1 x carrot
1 x white onion
2 x celery stalks
4 x garlic cloves

BBQ SAUCE

300g ketchup
4 tbsp Worcestershire sauce
1 tbsp wholegrain mustard
½ tsp paprika
1 tsp soy sauce
3 tbsp light brown sugar

METHOD

FOR THE SAUCE

Put all of the ingredients in a pan and bring them slowly to boiling point, reduce the temperature point and let them simmer for 3 - 4 minutes.

FOR THE RIBS

Season the ribs and put in the oven at 200ºC for 10 mins. This releases the fats and helps to brown the ribs. Then lower the temperature to 140ºC and cook for 3 hours. When the ribs are done (test for softness with a fork) pour over the BBQ sauce and return to the oven for 10 minutes whilst whacking up the temperature to 200 again. By putting the sauce in at this time it doesn't burn but retains all of its flavour.

VISIT THE HALF BUTT

Great Horkesley, Colchester CO6 4ET

www.thehalfbutt.co.uk

FOR THE SWEET POTATO WEDGES

Just before you do the final stage of the ribs, peel four sweet potatoes and chop into wedges. Brush with a little oil, sprinkle with a little salt and pepper. If you like paprika, shake over a dusting and then pop in the oven for 20 mins. When done, plate up and sprinkle a tiny amount of sea salt and thyme for seasoning.

NOW IT'S YOUR TURN!

Cook Lucasz's 'Rack of Ribs' and upload a picture of your dish to Instagram @thechefschallenge.

Next up... NORTH HILL NOODLE BAR

The next chef up to the pass is my old friend Leon.

More often than not, when I deliver Leon's cooking oil to him, he asks me to try the next new thing he has been cooking (his curries, by the way, are scrumptious!) and it is always a flavour sensation. For this book he has offered one of his simplest and yet tastiest dishes. It is sort of easy to cook but difficult to get right. Crispy squid.

THE CHEF

Leon Hee (English) Joon Fah Hee (Malaysian) comes from Malaysia, Kuala Lumpur and was born into a family of cooks and caterers. Many of his amazing recipes are based on his family's 'street food' influences. He moved to the UK when he was 26 to join friends here and to improve his cookery skills. He is well established at The North Hill Noodle Bar in Colchester, and is now aiming to create more menus that bring Western and Asian cooking together.

The Noodle bar was an instant hit when it started out 20 years ago, and continues to fill its tables with locals and foodies alike. People frequently ask the staff how this or that dish is prepared and cooked, and Leon's simple but amazingly tasty crispy squid is one of those often asked for.

THE DISH

Crispy hot and spicy squid to serve 2 people..

INGREDIENTS

200g squid tubes
1 medium beaten egg (or two medium eggs with egg white only if you want the batter colour to have no yellow shade to it at all)
100g of corn flour
1/2 teaspoon of five spice
1/2 teaspoon of salt
1/2 teaspoon of white pepper
Chopped garlic
Chopped chillies
Chopped spring onions
Veg oil (amount depends on size of saucepan as long as it's enough to cover 2" deep)

METHOD

Cut squid into rectangular pieces and score zigzag pattern on one side (so they curl up when cooked).

Mix the squids in with egg.

Drain off excess of egg whites (you want just enough egg so it is enough to coat the squid) then put the squid in the bowl of corn flour seasoned with salt and white pepper (best to use a big deep mixing bowl

as the lightweight nature of cornflour might fly all over the place if the bowl is not deep enough!)

Make sure all squids are covered and appear powder dry (if the squids are still soggy that means either not enough cornflour or too much egg in the first place).

Dust off the excess cornflour and drop them individually into the saucepan with oil already heated up to approximately 180°C. Don't put too many of them in at once and make sure there is plenty of space in between them, so that all surfaces are in contact with hot oil. This will also will prevent them from dropping the temperature of the hot oil. If needs be, do 2 or 3 batches.

Fry for about 1-2 minutes.

(Tips: Take one out now and again. If the batter feels hard then it's ready. Don't forget, it's best to have the squid undercooked rather than overcooked as

chillies and spring onions with a little oil. Only for 10 sec or so (don't overcook them as you still want then relatively crunchie) then drop all the squids in. Toss them a couple of times and then sprinkle the flavour mix (five spice, salt and pepper) over them. You won't need that much, just use your fingers. You can also sprinkle some more to adjust taste.

Then serve.

VISIT NORTH HILL NOODLE BAR

2 North Hill, Colchester CO1 1DZ

www.northhillnoodlebar.co.uk

overcooked squid chews like rubber! So as soon as the batter is hard that's good enough. After all it is CRISPY chilli squid).

Leave the squid ideally on an elevated rack, if not then spread them out on a large plate with kitchen paper underneath (don't bunch them together otherwise they start sweating and become soggy).

In a separate wok/ frying pan, fry the chopped garlic,

NOW IT'S YOUR TURN!

Cook Leon's 'Crispy Hot Squid' and upload a picture of your dish to Instagram @thechefschallenge.

Next up... THE ANGEL

THE ANGEL, KELVEDON

The next chef up to the pass is Luke Taylor from The Angel in Kelvedon, and Luke's top tip is really worth taking note of as it is repeated it over and over by other chefs.

Luke is one of my oldest customers and as such is an old friend. He is very passionate about using local suppliers to him, such as The Little Fish shop in Kelvedon and Fairfield Farm potatoes as well as having their crisps on sale. Actually, a lot of my local chefs use Fairfield Farm products, and if you get to know Laura and Robert who run Fairfields farm you will know why; they are obsessive about quality and a lovely couple t'boot! Get to know your local suppliers is Luke's advice, and I agree.

THE CHEF

Luke Taylor grew up in Rayne Braintree. After he left school, he already knew that he wanted to be a chef having developed a love of cooking from home. He attended Braintree College and studied a GNVQ Advanced Catering & Hospitality. His catering career started as a Kitchen Assistant at Pizza Hut (got to get used to being in a high pressured kitchen!).

From there his journey started to flourish, and he became a commis chef at Felstead School. From there his career began to blossom in earnest. To broaden his skills he moved, as many chefs do, to work at a variety of establishments such as Colchester United Football Ground and The Donkey & Buskins in Layer De La Haye gaining valuable experience and knowledge. He then worked his way up to Chef De Partie, then Sous Chef and eventually Head Chef. He joined The Angel in Kelvedon 3 years ago, but lives in Colchester now with his wife and their 8-year-old Jack Russell.

THE DISH

Pan-fried sun-dried tomato and parmesan herb crusted cod loin with sauté new potatoes, olives, green beans & spinach.

INGREDIENTS

4 X cod loin pieces 250g each (supplied by The Little Fish Shop of Kelvedon)
800g cooked new potatoes
120g capers
120g olives
80g baby spinach
40g dried breadcrumbs
40g grated parmesan
40g sun-dried tomatoes
40g green beans
I x lemon
1 X bunch of dill
Pinch of smoked paprika
Salt and pepper to season
Olive oil to fry
Balsamic glaze

METHOD

Pre heat the oven to 200°C Gas Mark 6.

In a food processor, blitz together the dried breadcrumbs, grated parmesan, some dill and sun-dried tomatoes, use the juice from the sun-dried tomatoes and a little olive oil to bind it all together, this will form the crust for the dish.

Place frying pan on hob, once hot, add olive oil, fry the white side of the fish until it starts getting a nice golden colour, turn the pieces of fish over on to the skin side, Lightly season with salt and pepper and a little smoked paprika, then add the crust by lightly pressing onto the fish and place into the pre-heated oven and cook for about 10 to 12 minutes.

cod on top, dress with balsamic glaze and garnish with lemon wedge and dill.

VISIT THE ANGEL

St Mary's Square, Kelvedon, Colchester CO5 9AN

www.theangelkelvedon.com

After 5 minutes of the fish being in the oven, place a wok on the hob and, once hot, add a little olive oil and the juice from the sun-dried tomato. Chef tip: this adds extra depth of flavour to the dish. Next, add the new potatoes and cook until they turn golden, then add the olives, capers, green beans and 4 lemon wedges, salt and pepper to season, add some dill and spinach and take off the heat.

Check cod is cooked. Chef tip: I use a cocktail stick, if it passes through the fish without the fish coming away on the stick then its cooked. Place the vegetable and caper mix in the centre of the plate and rest the

NOW IT'S YOUR TURN!

Cook Luke's 'Pan-Fried Cod' and upload a picture of your dish to Instagram @thechefschallenge.

Next up... KINGSFORD PARK

The next chef up to the pass is my dear friend Matt. I have known Matt for years and every time I deliver, he stops what he is doing for a chat and often a coffee. He once taught me how to make the most amazing piccalilli that put all other piccalilli's to shame!

THE CHEF

Mathew's journey in his own words:

Matthew Scully, South African at birth. I grew up experiencing great local and regional cuisine, from shore line caught seafood to Malabar curries. This opened my eyes to the world of possibilities working in the food industry.

I moved to the UK in 1993 and worked in different business sectors for years not knowing how to reach my calling; my desire to cook professionally for life. I managed to get into pro kitchens later on by working pro bono at weekends to learn my craft until eventually I took on a full-time position cooking for a living and haven't looked back!

I have cooked in pub kitchens, restaurants and large health spa resorts, and now also do private work from small intimate dinner parties to large catering operations.

I have a passion for using seasonal and fresh ingredients in all my recipes and am a strong advocate of farm to fork.

I am currently the Head Chef at Kingsford Park, Bannatyne Health Club and Apa. This dish is going to be on the menu from November until the end of February, ensuring that the produce is in season and at its prime.

THE DISH

Root vegetable biryani, and roti with lemon atchar.

INGREDIENTS (Serves 6)

LEMON ATCHAR (SOUTH ASIAN PICKLE)

1kg lemons
20g sea salt
500ml white wine vinegar
2 teaspoon crushed chillies
2 teaspoon mustard seeds
2 teaspoon curry powder
2 teaspoon whole coriander
1 star anise flower
10 teaspoon brown sugar

BIRYANI

500g parsnips
1/2 swede
1 small or 1/2 large Turnip
2 large carrots
1/2 Kohlrabi
1 Large red onions
1/4 tsp ground coriander
1/2 tsp Turmeric
1/4 tsp ground ginger
1/4 tsp mustard seeds
1 green chilli
2 cups basmati rice
5 cups vegetable stock
3 cloves garlic
4 cardamom pods
1/2 tsp cumin
1/4 bag fresh coriander
1/4 tsp cinnamon
Pinch of saffron
Vegetable oil

S, COLCHESTER

THE
CHEF'S CHALLENGE

METHOD

ATCHAR

3 or 4 days before making the dish, make the atchar. This gives time for the lemon skins to soften. Take about 9 lemons, wash and cut into quarters. Place into a container and sprinkle with 5 teaspoons coarse sea salt. Poor over 500ml white wine vinegar. Cover and leave for 36 hours. Then drain off any liquid that has accumulated. Make the atchar pickle by heating 250ml of good cold pressed rapeseed oil to 70°C (just above very warm) and adding the spices. The heat of the oil releases their flavours. Don't get your oil to hot or they will just burn. In a large bowl pour the oil over the lemons and mix until they are well coated. Pack into a jar and cover. Refrigerate.

BIRYANI

In a large bowl, peel and prepare the root vegetables into smallish cubes. Slice the white onions into strips. Finely chop the chillies and garlic.

Place the chilli, garlic and all the spices into a pan with the oil and start to heat through, add the onions and cook on low heat until soft.

Add the vegetables and stir through and add the stock and bring to a simmer and cook until softened.

In a separate pan cook the rice.

Once the vegetables have reduced place the rice on top with the saffron and bake in the oven for 20 minutes at 180°C.

ROTI RECIPE (MAKES 12)

270g plain flour (plus a little for dusting)

10ml rape seed oil

195ml water

Oil to brush the rotis

1 tsp black onion seeds

Put the flour, water, onion seeds and oil into the robo and blitz, remove and start to knead until a smooth texture is formed. Leave covered in the fridge for 2 hours.

Take out the dough and knead again, roll into a tube and cut 12 even portions. Flatten out with a roller and brush with oil the fry gently in a dry pan on both sides until lightly browned in patches.

VISIT KINGSFORD PARK

Kingsford Park, Layer Rd, Colchester CO2 0HS

spa.bannatyne.co.uk/colchester-kingsford-park

NOW IT'S YOUR TURN!

Cook Matt's 'Biryani, Roti & Atchar' and upload a picture of your dish to Instagram @thechefschallenge.

Next up, THE FORESTERS

The next chef up to the pass is Louise Parkin of The Foresters.

THE CHEF

I have known Louise for years and have seen her develop her cooking skills exponentially. Louise is a lady with a ready smile and an incredibly well organised mind, and the reason I can say that is that she works in such a small kitchen that to knock out 35 to 50 covers one has to be very well organised.

Lou's story:

Born in Bedford in 1967, my parents moved to Mersea Island when I was seven. I went to a small boarding school just outside Norwich at the age of nine. As a child, I wanted to be everything from a vet to an artist, but ended up working in my local pub as a waitress. I did a YTS (youth training scheme) at The Tudor Halt on East Hill (now the Curve Bar). I worked in many of the hotels and bars around the town. I then moved around a bit, and then came back, and have lived in Colchester for 23 years.

I attended Colchester Institute and Anglia Ruskin University and did a degree in Environmental Monitoring and Protection. I then worked for the local authority in Environmental Health for 12 years. I left the Authority in early 2013, and immediately started a patisserie course at Colchester Institute and enjoyed the course so much that I applied to do the professional

cookery course as well.

The course was fascinating and I was quite emotional when it all came to an end and I finished. I had already started working at the Foresters Arms part time and then had my first placement at The Victory at Mersea through the summer of 2014.

This was a different kettle of fish altogether, from a small kitchen, literally a cupboard under the stairs with a lean-to attached, working mostly alone, to working with six chefs and hundreds of covers a day. I did two years at The Foresters running the kitchen, and then after a fabulous trip to America, I did ten months at the Lexden Crown working with several chefs. I took a break for some months and then in February 2019 I went to The Old Siege House to work for Darren Lisney; he had been going to teach me in my last year at Colchester Institute but had opened this restaurant instead. In March 2020, I was furloughed from the Siege House, and in late August found myself back in the cupboard under the stairs at the Foresters Arms.

THE DISH.

The Foresters Beef and Oyster Pie (Serves 6)

THE INGREDIENTS.

THE PIE FILLING

500g Stewing steak, diced

1 large carrot

3 medium onions

1 pint Colchester Brewery London porter (we also use Sweeny Tod)

1 tbsp balsamic vinegar

2 bay leaves

2 sprigs of thyme

Salt and pepper

6 oysters

The pastry

SUET PASTRY

300g plain flour

100g unsalted butter

100g beef suet

Pinch of salt and white pepper

Water

1 egg, beaten

POTATO, CELERIAC AND MUSTARD MASH

300g celeriac

500g white potatoes

Knob of butter

Splash of cream

Tsp English mustard

Pinch salt and pepper

THE CARROTS

Big carrots!

THE GRAVY

1 pint Beef stock

1 medium onion

1 bottle Colchester Porter

Juice of half a lemon

1 tsp sugar

Cornflour

THE METHOD

Remember to make the mix and maybe the pastry the day before cooking and assembling the dish if you can.

1) Preheat oven to 160°C

2) Sweat onion and carrot in large frying pan till soft and golden, pour into casserole dish.

3) In the large frying pan then brown the meat in batches, add to casserole, add a heaped dessert spoon of cornflour to the last batch and cook, any fat should be soaked up by the cornflour and this will help to thicken the sauce when it cooks with the beer and the balsamic.

4) Put the mixture into a heavy based saucepan and pour in the beer, balsamic vinegar and herbs. Cover the meat with a little water and bring to the boil.

5) Put on the lid and into the oven. Cook for 3.5 hrs, check to ensure it doesn't dry out then allow the mixture to cool. The pie mixture can be made the day before, in any event it will need time to cool.

6) Make pastry, mix all dry ingredients, rub in butter and suet until it resembles breadcrumbs. and add enough water to hold the paste together, do not overwork the pastry. Wrap in cling film and

7) Make your pie/s.

8) Shuck your oysters, keep them cool and ensure there is no shell or grit in them. N.B If you have never 'shucked' an oyster before (opening one) there are many tutorials online. Failing that, ask your fishmonger to shuck them for you.

9) Once the beef stew is cool, roll out 2/3 of your pastry to 1/2 cm thick and place into a prepared pie dish, let it rest for 20 minutes. This will avoid your pastry shrinking during cooking. (Lou uses Bakery Direct 100 Round Silver Pukka Pie foils/Dishes from Amazon, just as a size measure.)

10) Roll out the rest of the pastry for the lid.

11) Generously fill your pie/s with your beef casserole, place the oysters on top, one per pie, make the pies 'domed'.

12) Place the pie lid over the top, trim and crimp the edges, you can make a decoration with the trimmings of the pastry if you want to, at the foresters I use a Xmas tree cutter to represent the Foresters. Egg-wash the pastry.

13) Place in the oven for 35-40 minutes or until the pastry is golden brown and cooked through.

14) For the porter gravy, chop the onion and fry to soft and golden, add the porter, reduce by a half, add beef stock reduce by a third.

15) Thicken with cornflour slurry (That's cornflour and cold water in equal measure, usually about a level dessert spoon of cornflour and one of water.)

16) Adjust the flavour, if the gravy is too bitter add some lemon juice and sweeten with a spoon of brown sugar.

17) Peel and boil your potatoes, mash them.

18) Peel and dice celeriac, boil till soft, mash them, or blitz them in a food processor.

19) mash together potatoes, celeriac, butter, cream

and mustard. Season well with salt and white pepper.

20) Place whole carrots in a roasting dish with vegetable oil, season and add herbs and garlic to taste. Place in a medium oven and roast till you can just push a knife through them. Cut into large slices to serve.

21) Plate up and serve.

VISIT THE FORESTERS

1-2 Castle Rd, Colchester CO1 1UW

www.theforestersarms.co.uk/

NOW IT'S YOUR TURN!

Cook Lou's 'Beef and Oyster Pie' and upload a picture of your dish to Instagram @thechefschallenge.

Next up... THE SWAN

A NOTE ON INGREDIENTS

The message from every chef in this book is to source your ingredients locally if and when you can. This is not just about supporting local business, but also just finding some elusive ingredients can be its own adventure. We are lucky where we live to have Coleman's of Boxted as our butchers, just a stone's throw away, and I love going there because they really know their stuff. If I am unsure about what cut of meat to use in a recipe, they will give me the best advice and I'm pretty sure that your local butcher will be the same.

We are also lucky to have 'The Little Fish Shop' just down the A12 in Kelvedon and whatever I can't get in a supermarket they can get from Billingsgate market, so not only do they have a great range of fish ready to go they are also able to source fish that might be unusual or difficult to get from supermarkets. If there are no fishmongers near you, check out delivery companies like Palmers Fish home delivery service (found on Facebook).

Get to know your local breweries as well because beer, for me at least, is an essential cooking ingredient in many a dish and we are lucky enough in this country to have had an explosive growth of microbreweries over the last ten years. The Colchester Brewing Company is our local and does a fine range of beers but there is also The St Botolph's Brewery and many others; search out the breweries closest to you and give them a try, and I bet you will find people passionate about their products.

Local veg shops and farmers markets are also adventures by themselves. When you go to buy veg, go without a watch and take your time (couldn't resist that one!). When you start to research veg shops, you'll be surprised at the variety of products that they sell and the in-depth knowledge that they have about their produce. Locally grown and locally sourced also means that they will have a great understanding of what's in season and what's coming next.

Don't get me wrong, supermarkets are great places with a wide range of stuff and I shop weekly at ours. But if you want expert knowledge, then search out the local producers and wholefood shops. What an amazing age we live in that we can just tap into a computer, phone or tablet to find anything that we need (always being able to afford that is a different thing for us, depending on how close pay day is though!) So, remember to use the search engines to find what you need and to get the tips on cooking. Personally, I am addicted to BBC Good Food, which has a wealth of recipes that I often use to compare what I am cooking with what they are saying.

THE CHEF

The next chef up to the pass is Benjamin Morgan from The Swan in Long Melford.

As the newly appointed chef at The Swan, Ben is also new to me but I got to know him quite well during the photo shoot and he is a chef with natural instinct; you can see it when you watch him cook and feel it when he talks about food and how one should be with the other chefs when one is in charge.

It was a photo shoot that I loved doing because of the atmosphere in the kitchen. The K.P. was joking with chefs, and the waitresses were smiling and laughing when they came into the kitchen – two sure signs that the Head Chef knows what he is doing. I can say that because I have been going into kitchens for years, and you just get a feel for when there is someone in charge who 'gets it'. Ben gets it.

Ben, in his own words:

"My name's Ben and I've been a chef for the last 14 years. I was born and bred in Suffolk and I've always chosen to work in small pub-restaurants in the area. I think Suffolk produces some of the best food and drink, and I really enjoy creating dishes from local produce."

Ben is short on words but big on talent and very self-effacing as you can see. You are going to love his dish, it's a flavour sensation!

THE DISH

Pan fried hake, cauliflower dahl, spiced onion bhaji and pickled vegetables.

INGREDIENTS & METHOD

FOR THE DAHL

1 cauliflower

1 fennel bulb

1 lemongrass

1 red chilli

1 shallot

1 clove of garlic

1 teaspoon mild curry powder

2 teaspoons cumin (ground)

1 teaspoon ginger (ground)

300ml veg stock

1 tin coconut cream

Salt to taste

Sweat down vegetables on low heat, until soft and add spices, cook out for 2-3 minutes, add veg stock, reduce by 3/4, add coconut cream and simmer for 1 minute gently, remove from heat.

FOR THE BHAJI

2 onions

1 egg

200g self raising flour

50g desiccated coconut

2 teaspoons curry powder

10g sesame seeds

10g black onion seeds

5 g salt

Mix all ingredients together in large mixing bowl, spoon 25g portions into deep fat fryer, cook at 160oC until golden brown.

FOR THE HAKE

160g portions

Pan fry the hake 2 ½ minutes either side in a table spoon of olive or cold pressed rapeseed oil and 25 grams of butter then rest for one minute.

For the pickled veg

2 shallots diced

8 radishes diced

2 carrots diced

The Liquor.

200ml white wine vinegar

40g salt

60g sugar

6 cardamom pods

20 black peppercorns

1 teaspoon cumin seeds

1 teaspoon coriander seeds

Slide the vegetables thinly into julienne (cut into matchsticks), leave in heatproof tub. Bring pickle liquor and spices to the boil, pour over vegetables, let them cool and leave in the fridge for 24 hours before serving.

PLATING

The dahl goes down first to create a base flavour, then place the bhaji's (2 per plate) next to the dahl and place the hake onto the dahl to one side and add a few pickled veg to the other side. Enjoy!

VISIT THE SWAN

Hall St, Long Melford, Sudbury CO10 9JQ

www.longmelfordswan.co.uk

NOW IT'S YOUR TURN!

Cook Ben's 'Pan Fried Hake' and upload a picture of your dish to Instagram @thechefschallenge.

Next up, BRADFIELD COMBUST

THE CHEF

Richard is one of those chefs who always smiles and always has a moment to chat. That is really important in a chef who is part of an amazing team. I have been servicing The Manger for over a year, and watched its new owners John and Carolyn build it up against all the odds. They built their team from Richard down; The Manger now has an enviable reputation of serving locally sourced and freshly prepared food in a particularly friendly atmosphere.

It shows how good the chef and that team are because The Manger, a 15th century, beamed, dog-friendly coaching inn between Bury St Edmunds and Sudbury is in the middle of nowhere, which means people specifically choose to go there, rather than are just passing trade. That, for me, is the mark of great food and great hosts. I love the place.

Richard himself began working as a pot washer (some years ago) but started taking on all the jobs that the chefs didn't want to do themselves like cleaning fish and zesting! He was eventually asked if he would like to train up and gain his City and Guilds in London, and he jumped at the chance. Since then, he has gone from strength to strength working at such places as The Serpentine in Hyde Park, HMS Belfast, Westminster Abbey and even Bentleys in Sudbury.

THE DISH

Vegan shepherds pie.

INGREDIENTS (SERVES 6)

500gms sweet potatoes

500gms Maris Piper potatoes

100gms diced onions

100gms green lentils

100gms diced celery

200gms diced carrots

100gms diced leeks

200gms diced butternut squash

150gms diced red pepper

125gms diced button mushrooms

400gms tin chopped tomatoes

400gms tin mixed beans

3 garlic cloves

50ml rapeseed oil

500ml cold water

Salt, pepper and fresh oregano to season

THE METHOD

Peel both the Maris Piper and sweet potatoes. Chop and boil in the same pan. When soft season to taste with salt and pepper. Mash together and leave to cool.

Boil green lentils from 500ml cold water for 30 minutes.

Sweat off diced onions, diced celery, diced carrots, diced leeks and diced butternut squash in 50ml rapeseed oil for 10 minutes. Add diced red pepper, diced button mushrooms and 3 crushed garlic cloves.

Add chopped tomatoes and mixed beans. Season with fresh oregano. Mix thoroughly. Simmer for 2 minutes.

VISIT THE MANGER

The Street, Bradfield Combust, Bury Saint Edmunds IP30 0LW

www.themanger.online

Fill serving dish, leave to cool.

Once cool top with the mashed Maris Piper and sweet potato.

Pre-cook for 40 minutes at 180 degrees

Serve with fresh vegetables (broccoli, fine beans and cauliflower as a suggestion) and vegan gravy.

NOW IT'S YOUR TURN!

Cook Richard's 'Vegan Shepherd's Pie' and upload a picture of your dish to Instagram @thechefschallenge.

Next up... STATION ROAD

The next chef up to the pass is Nathan Hellyer from Station Road.

THE CHEF

I only met Nathan a month or so ago, and yet I have been servicing Station road for a long time. The place was taken over by some guys that I have known for a long time and who are very talented chefs, but a tad shy to publicity, so here I shall name them and shame the Devil; they are Liam Liskus and Aran Henderson. Aran talks at a hundred miles an hour and thinks twice as fast, I struggle to keep up! Both are chefs with a long history of achievements and a wealth of experience and skills.

These two guys are hugely talented, but have given the helm over to Nathan so they must believe in him big time and, after the photo shoot I did with him, I agree with their trust in him; he is an awesome chef and is providing a dish that is hugely simple and, yet, at the same time really tricky to get right. It has defeated many a professional chef, but now it's your turn to try cooking the Tomahawk Steak!

There are two ways that chefs become Head Chefs and beyond, and both are valid ways of learning the trade. Either they train at a college or similar, or they learn their trade by showing their passion and rising through the ranks by experience. Nathan is definitely rising through the ranks and has soaked up the lessons of his craft by working at such places as The

Henny Swan and The Essex Golf and Country Club. These are places that demand a high standard of skill and also offer chefs a great opportunity to learn their crafts. Nathan has most definitely learned his. He has a huge range of dishes but he is offering this Tomahawk Steak out to you as I asked him to set you a big challenge and that is exactly what he has done!

THE DISH

They don't call this the Tomahawk for nothing! This is a steak that will feed four people and the dog down the road, but if cooked right will be one of the best steaks that you will ever eat. Also, there are no amounts for ingredients here so you are going to have to wing it...

INGREDIENTS

Tomahawk steak

Chestnut mushrooms

Double cream

Vine cherry tomatoes

Truffle oil

Rosemary

Salt

Pepper

Maris Piper potatoes

Rocket

Red onion

Veg oil

METHOD

Begin by taking your tomahawk out of the fridge and allowing it to rest fully, coming to room temperature.

Preheat your oven to 170 degrees.

Season with rosemary, salt, and pepper.

Whilst this is resting, prepare your accoutrements.

Slice a Maris Piper potato into chunky chip size and wash in cold water, before leaving in a bowl of cold water to soak. This helps to get rid of the starch.

Slice a handful of chestnut mushrooms into thin slices and leave to one side.

Prepare your red onion and rocket salad, this can then be left in the fridge until ready to serve.

Preheat some high smoke point oil in a pan on your stove top until approximately 170-190 degrees.

Drain your chips, and pat thoroughly dry, before placing in your preheated oil on your stove top. Be careful as hot oil is liable to spit when in contact with water.

Now, once the steak has been adequately rested, heat your grill top until smoking hot, and put a little high smoke point oil on your steak.

Place on your grill top, hearing the heated sizzle when you do, and allow 4-5 minutes on each side, in order to get a nice crust.

Once a nice crust has developed, place in your preheated oven for 20-25 minutes.

Whilst this is cooking, heat up a pan and add your mushrooms, minced garlic, and truffle oil. Allow some of the water from the mushrooms to dissipate before adding your double cream and allowing to reduce for 10-15 minutes.

Take your vine tomatoes and place in the oven alongside your steak for 5 minutes, before finishing sharply on the hot grill top, or with a kitchen blowtorch, should you have one.

Once the time allotted has passed, take your steak out and, adding a knob of butter to the top, allow to rest for 10-15 minutes.

Get your board (or plate) and slice your tomahawk to your personal preference, making sure to remove the long bone first of all.

Further garnish your serving dish, with your salad, chips and tomato's, before spooning your truffle mushroom sauce over the top.

Bon Appetit.

VISIT STATION ROAD

10 Station Road, Sudbury, Suffolk CO10 2SS

www.facebook.com/station.road.sudbury/

The next chef up at the pass is Nick from The Crown at Stoke by Nayland.

THE CHEF

Nick has a passion for food and loves his job but his real passion is for bringing on new chefs and giving them opportunities to shine. I have known Nick for some time now and can say that he really knows how to run a great kitchen. Like some of the places I visit (not all) the kitchen is a vibrant living thing of its own with everyone knowing exactly what is expected of them and more. The constantly full car park attests to the popularity of the food and staff at The Crown.

It comes as no surprise to me because I've seen the list of places he has worked at, such as The renowned Ivy, and other top chefs that he has worked with including Angela Hartnett at The York and Albany in London. Nick's credentials are undeniable and his food sublime. Here he gives us his take on the simplest of dishes and yet for me one of the tastiest. If you were put off liver and bacon by your grandma's chewy lump boiled with onions it is time for you to re-think the dish. This one is awesome!

THE DISH.

Pan fried calves' liver, smoked back bacon, garlic mash, crispy kale, wild mushroom & port sauce.

INGREDIENTS

2 thick slices of calves' liver app 180g

2 slices back bacon (skinned and trimmed)

Prepped wild mushrooms 60g

1 portion mash with a teaspoon of garlic puree and plenty of butter (to your taste).

Small handful of kale deep fried, drained on a paper towel and seasoned.

Port sauce.

THE PORT SAUCE

1 shallot finely chopped

2 cloves of Garlic finely chopped and crushed

200ml Beef stock

300ml Port

1 tbs red wine vinegar

2 tsp redcurrant jelly

METHOD

In a saucepan, gently fry the onions and garlic until pungent.

Add beef stock and reduce by have on a simmer.

Add the port, vinegars and red current jelly and simmer for 15 mins then strain through a sieve. (5 mins less time simmering for a thinner sauce, 5 mins more time simmering for a thicker sauce.)

VISIT THE CROWN

Park St, Stoke-by-Nayland, Colchester CO6 4SE

www.crowninn.net

THE METHOD

Warm the mash up with the garlic.

Deep fry the Kale for 30 seconds until crisp, leave to cool.

Get a large frying pan to heat, small amount of oil.

Start with the pan nearly smoking.

Fry the bacon first, then fry the liver very quickly, 2 minutes on each side.

Add the mushrooms to pan.

Remove liver and bacon and finish mushrooms in port sauce.

Mash on plate, then liver and bacon and mushrooms, finish with the sauce and kale.

NOW IT'S YOUR TURN!

Cook Nick's 'Pan Fried Calves' Liver' and upload a picture of your dish to Instagram @thechefschallenge.

Next up... THE GRANARY

Last but not least, our final chef up to the pass is Chris from The Granary at Waldegraves.

THE CHEF

I have been servicing The Granary at Waldegraves now for well over three years and have watched it grow steadily in popularity with people on and off of Mersea Island. During that time, I have watched a few chefs come and go, but Chris being the backbone of the place has always been around and under his guidance the place has just gone from strength to strength, this comes as no surprise when you hear his own story.

"I started in the catering trade a week away from my 14th birthday when mum came home from her job and said they needed someone to wash the glasses tomorrow night at the local pub where she worked. I immediately was hooked.

I quickly progressed from glass wash, into the kitchen and that is where it started. I remember probably in 1977, Geoff the chef took me into his bubble and taught me the basics. This was in a pub in Highcliffe, Dorset managed by my future in laws who were really the people who taught me my ethics in the restaurant trade that I now adopt.

They encouraged me on leaving school to enrol at Bournemouth Catering College, which I left in 1980 after completing what was then Chef City & Guilds

706/1/2/3, Hotel Diploma, Chef of the Term, and quite a few other awards. I also spent three months being tutored by Brian Turner at the Capital Hotel, Knightsbridge in London. He offered me a position at the hotel, but I declined, stayed with my then to-be wife and embarked on the pub trail.

I quickly went into pub management and was lucky to be very successful, increasing turnover at the businesses I took hold of and winning various awards over the years.

I also spent four years catering for VIP business flights and airlines, plus kings, queens, princes, football teams, and pop stars out of Stansted Airport.

The Granary Bar & Restaurant is situated on Waldegraves Holiday Park, Mersea Island. I was asked on arrival to the business to open a restaurant on the park, and I have now developed The Granary into a destination that welcomes many returning customers

My ethic...

There's only one way to do a job and that is the right way, therefore you do not have to do it again."

THE DISH

Pork loin with brandy and peppercorn sauce.

INGREDIENTS

2 x 4oz pork loin steaks

FOR THE MASH

50g butter

200g potato mash

Whole grain mustard

2 X carrots

1 X parsnip

Honey

4 sprigs fresh thyme

FOR THE SAUCE

50g finely diced shallots

Cracked & whole peppercorns

25ml brandy

25ml white wine

100ml beef stock

150ml double cream

Peel and cut the carrots and parsnips to chunky lengths, blanch lightly in boiling water till slightly soft.

Put into a small roasting tray, season and cover with the honey and add the thyme.

Add grain mustard, to your liking to the potato mash and mix, keep warm

In a saute pan melt the butter, add the pork steaks, season with salt and pepper, and cook for approximately 8 minutes, turning and coating regularly. When cooked through, remove from the pan and leave to rest.

Pour the juices from the pan over the carrots and parsnips, and put into the oven for 5 minutes turning frequently.

In the same pan, add a knob of butter, melt, and add the diced onion, peppercorns, and saute for 3 minutes. Add the brandy and wine, saute till reduced to one third quantity. Add the stock and reduce again to one quarter quantity, then add the cream and reduce till a nice consistency. Season with a pinch of sea salt.

To serve, spoon the mustard mash onto the plate, place the loin steaks leaning, garnish with the parsnips and carrots, pour over the pepper sauce.

VISIT THE GRANARY

Waldegraves Ln, West Mersea, Colchester CO5 8SE

www.waldegraves.co.uk/holiday-activities/ mersea-restaurants/

NOW IT'S YOUR TURN!

Cook Chris's 'Pork Loin' and upload a wture of your dish to Instagram @thechefschallenge.

If you're a restaurant or chef, and would like to take part in a future Chef's Challenge book – or have a bespoke book created for your establishment – just email me at djcatrell@hotmail.com.

ACKNOWLEDGEMENTS

With thanks to all the chefs who took part, to my family for their support, and to Cara Thurlbourn for editing, publishing, and designing this book.

IMAGE ACKNOWLEDGEMENTS

Photography by D J Cattrell

Stock photography: Nadine Preimeau, Heather Ford, Christian Mackie, NordWood Themes, and Calum Lewis from Unsplash.com